Kick-Start

*Realizing Best Benefits from a Science,
Technical or Business Internship*

John M Newsam

Printed in the United States of America
First Printing, 2018
ISBN-13: 978-1727469578
ISBN-10: 1727469577

Cover artwork was designed by Bill Hinsch
of Learning Visuals, www.LearningVisualsCS.com

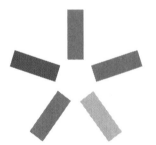

Casa de Colibrí Productions
528 Forward Street
La Jolla CA 92037-7528
www.casadecolibri.com

Table of Contents

Introduction

I have not been in a position identical to any of the students who has interned with me to date. Before beginning postgraduate research I had a wide variety of temporary jobs, including milk delivery hand, mobile vegetable store assistant, laborer in an orange juice packing company and on a hop and fruit farm in Kent, grouse-beater in the moors of Angus, Scotland, as temporary worker at a central post office over the Christmas rush, running a mobile DJ business, selling festival publications on the streets of Edinburgh, and making and selling decorative candles. The goal of all these jobs was immediate income. They each also provided a learning experience to some degree, but that was certainly not the primary purpose at the time.

My recent work as an internship mentor and supervisor (and the basis for most of the experiences mentioned here) has taken place in San Diego, California. The experiences and examples also conform with a reasonably tight demographical cross-section. Most of the internship programs have involved undergraduates or recent graduates from San Diego colleges and universities, with a smaller number from local high schools.

I was also very fortunate that the first intern with whom I had the opportunity to work, who was then a high school student in New Jersey, was truly exceptional.

Few, if any, of the internships that I have supervised offered the possibility of a longer-term engagement for the intern. Connecting with a capable individual early in their career, one who might later become an employee or a colleague, though, has always been part of the appeal to me of my mentoring commitment.

I continue to work to further improve my own approach to internships. I had outlined the principles I now follow to several colleagues, but I had no thought to formally document my approach. That is, until a close friend, Dr. John Chiplin, suggested that I should write a book on the subject. Here it is.

In the subsequent text, "host" refers to the organization engaging the intern, "supervisor" refers to the intern's manager in that organization, and "mentor" refers to an individual who serves as a trusted counselor and role model to the intern. Typically, the supervisor is also the primary mentor.

I would be interested to receive any and all feedback, relative not only to format, but also to the content and to omissions.

John M Newsam, San Diego 2018

Internship

What is an internship and what is special about it?

An internship is a temporary trainee position in a host organization, paid or unpaid.

The primary intent is for the intern to gain practical work experience and knowledge in a particular work sector. Successful completion of the internship will then position the intern favorably for subsequent employment in that sector.

There is a reasonable expectation of benefit to both intern and host organization. In return for providing training and sharing certain domain knowledge with the intern, the host organization realizes some measure of extra labor and potentially other benefits.

An internship is typically of 2-4 months duration. The upper end of the bell curve on duration extends to perhaps a year and the lower to as short as 2 weeks.

As the emphasis is on training, an intern is typically an early career professional seeking either a basis for informed career direction decisions, or credentials that will subsequently facilitate gaining employment.

Appeal to Intern

Why should I seek an internship?

Completing one or more internships is highly recommended for the current student or recent graduate. There are several reasons why.

Academic Credit

Several academic institutions offer courses for which all or part of the curriculum entails successful completion of an industrial internship. Usually, such courses have a documented set of requirements. An internship might have a defined duration, a mechanism of oversight and review by a faculty member, and the expectation of closeout completion in the form of a presentation or report.

The requirements will typically provide for confidential information of the hosting company being protected, even if the intern has exposure to such information while working.

Experience for the Resume

When an applicant has relevant practical experience the appeal of the applicant's resume to a recruiter is increased. A resume reviewer will consider job experiences, including internships, and an interviewer will likely ask about such experience. Even where the internship was in a field not directly related to the position now being sought, the work experience will be viewed positively.

Possible Future Employment

Several organizations will hire a prospective new employee first as an intern to ascertain whether the individual indeed suits the intended position. Even if there is no such expectation at the outset, if the intern performs creditably, should an employee position be or become available the intern will be positioned well as a candidate.

Recommendations

Establishing a professional interaction through an internship obligates the host organization or, more especially, the mentor and supervisor, to provide recommendations and references should the intern seek subsequent employment somewhere else. A proactive mentor will also scout for opportunities for an intern and, likely, be pleased to maintain an ongoing professional interaction.

Networking and Introductions

An individual early in their career will typically have only a limited professional network. In social networks such as LinkedIn that facilitate making new connections with second- or third-level links, an intern will realize a substantial benefit when becoming part of a mentor's network.

Conversancy with Possible Career Directions

Most established professionals will point to no more than a handful of pivotal decision points in their own career progression. Any such decision will benefit from being best informed. An intern has the chance to learn about the spectrum of job types and career directions possible within the type of organization represented by the host.

This 'testing of the waters' is more difficult outside of an internship. Terminating or being terminated from an employee position within three years of being hired is generally inadvisable. An internship has a commitment period of only as short as some weeks.

Practical Exposure

For a non-vegetarian, sea urchin can be somewhat of an acquired taste. If you have never tasted sea urchin, how do you know whether you will like it? Until one has been immersed in the day-to-day mechanics for a period, it is hard to know whether a given professional role or work environment affords personal resonance. An internship is a vehicle for sampling a given position, even if at a relatively low responsibility level. It also provides an opportunity to interact with employees in other roles and to develop informed perspectives also on those other types of position.

Compensation

Even the modest compensation for an internship that is paid will help pay the bills.

Lower Bar

Recruiting an intern can be less laborious for a company and, concomitantly, it can be easier to be engaged as an intern rather than as a formal employee. An internship entails a lower level of commitment for both intern and host.

Benefit to Host

Why should a host organization engage an intern?

If structured and managed appropriately, the aggregate returns to the host should outweigh the costs.

Exploring New Avenues
Particularly for a volunteer internship, applied to a project that would otherwise be unaddressed, the intern serves as a resource to explore a new scientific, technical or engineering concept, or to explore a novel prospective business dimension.

Help with the Work Load
An intern can usually be identified and engaged readily, without any of the machinations that might be required to hire an employee. The costs of engagement can be low. An internship on a paid basis can be a swift means of adding extra staff.

There are risks. An intern will develop a level of competence and familiarity with the work, which will then be lost when the internship ends.

Satisfying a Desire to Reciprocate
Many professionals, recognizing the benefits that they themselves realized from earlier mentoring and work experience, will likely be enthusiastic to 'give back', to provide to an early career individual benefits similar to those that they had themselves realized.

Cementing a Relationship
Engaging an intern from an institution, or from the group of a faculty member at the institution, will help build further the relationship with the institution or the faculty.

Favor for a Friend

Should a professional colleague or friend in the technical or business community ask that a prospective intern be considered, they will undoubtedly be given consideration. Concomitantly, the colleague will be eager to return the favor.

Student Request

The motivation to further build relationships is not directed solely to senior professionals, but also to capable individuals earlier in the careers. A mentor will be interested to support a student who has performed well in a class taught by the mentor. A host will be eager to establish links with peers of a student who has previously completed an internship successfully.

Fresh Enthusiasm

An intern will be 'new blood' in a group or small company, bringing fresh perspectives which can be beneficial, even should they be somewhat naïve. Someone who is unfamiliar with the company activities or modus operandi can be an encouragement to the employee base, even helping each staff member to appreciate their own level of knowledge and experience.

Additional Hands

An intern will typically have relatively junior standing. The intern might have sufficient flexibility in their schedule to contribute to social activities, or to volunteer outreach efforts, such as participation in science fairs or festivals, career visits, or discussions with other students interested in industry perspectives.

Network Expansion

An intern may serve as an entrée into an untapped networking domain. Whether the intern is engaged or not, the new networking connections might lead to further internship candidates in the future.

Small Company Perspective

What is special about a start-up or early phase company from an internship perspective?

Larger companies, those with more than some 250 employees, often have a formal internship program, such as offered over the summer period.

Only a limited number of small companies offer internships, and fewer still have formal programs.

However, an internship with a small company can be rewarding. The intern will be exposed to a broader array of job functions, is more likely to have responsibility for their own project and will have greater opportunity to impact the organization as a whole.

Several factors, though, may impede an early-phase or small company from engaging an intern.

The Thought to Engage an Intern Might Not Occur
The press of day-to-day operations may impede more strategic or creative planning.

No Experience of Engaging Interns
If the benefits are not recognized ahead of time as compelling and if no-one on the company team has experience of intern engagement there will be little motivation to consider such a possibility.

Limited Employee Bandwidth

Each member on an early-phase company team will have many more priorities on the 'to do' list than can be tackled in a given day. There may appear to be no time to apply to the process of engaging and supervising an intern.

Informal Structure and Organization

A small company may have but scant administrative support, requiring a prospective mentor to orchestrate a posting, application receipt, review, selection, interviewing and engagement process. Sufficient time may not be available.

Logistics to Streamline Engagement may not be in Place

Not having templates or documentation to support the recruitment and onboarding process, engagement of a first intern can be more laborious.

Concern Over Secrecy

Small companies have limited compartmentalization. Any staff member will be exposed to much of the company operations. This is a benefit to the intern, but the host organization needs to have confidence that this exposure does not come with an attendant risk of proprietary information being disseminated. If not properly briefed, an intern is unlikely to appreciate what types of information are sensitive, with an attendant risk of inadvertent disclosure.

Intern Hesitation

It may be more difficult to land a small company internship, so that a prospective intern will tend to gravitate towards larger companies, those that advertise formal programs, even though an internship with a startup might be a way of getting into an exciting endeavor at ground level.

Small Companies Often Miss Out

These concerns notwithstanding, many of the benefits to the host can be still more valuable for an early phase company. The precedent of engaging a first intern will likely establish a continuing pattern.

Unpaid or Paid

Why should I consider an unpaid internship position? Why might a host pay a stipend?

Both intern and host should expect to realize reasonable benefit from each internship project. The intangible benefits realized by the intern on an unpaid basis should be substantially greater than those realized on a paid basis.

Unpaid Basis

An internship undertaken on an unpaid basis must conform to labor law requirements.

Structured Project

The legal requirements on an unpaid internship are such that it is simplest to structure an unpaid internship around a specific project, one that the host organization would likely not otherwise undertake, or not undertake within an overlapping timeframe.

The project should be interesting both for the intern and for the host organization. There will likely be company policies and procedures to which the intern needs adhere, and background with which the intern needs to become familiar, but a project will be most valuable when the intern has a genuine sense of project ownership and responsibility.

The project will serve as a vehicle for the intern to accumulate experience, to learn more about working in a company, and to be exposed to various facets of the host organization. An appropriate project is designed such that completion is possible in the time available and is amenable to being summarized in a presentation upon completion.

Part Time

The majority of the unpaid internships supervised by the author have been part-time. An unpaid internship that is part-time, up to some 15-20 hours per week, permits an intern to have an additional part-time position that is paid. Such a job may be less rewarding professionally but can generate necessary income.

An internship that is part-time is also less likely to be construed as an employee position (such as under California labor law https://www.dir.ca.gov/dlse/FAQ_IndependentContractor.htm).

A prospective intern may agonize over their level of comfort in working at a for-profit organization on an unpaid basis. As with paying the costs of college, though, the amount that might otherwise have been received as compensation can be viewed as a sound investment in professional development.

Paid Basis

Menial Tasks

For several reasons, an internship on a paid basis is often not structured around a project devised specifically for the intern. Rather, the internship is viewed as a means of adding an extra pair of hands to help with one or more programs already underway. The intern will likely be assigned to more routine tasks

A small company will find it difficult to engage a paid intern for work in the laboratory that is anything other than menial, unless the candidate already has substantial laboratory experience and skills. Gaining familiarity with the host's laboratory procedures and quality systems might take several weeks, so that the intern begins to be productive only towards the end of the internship period.

The distinction between a temporary employee and a paid intern is blurred. From a human resources perspective, the host might consider the intern to be an employee. The intern would then be eligible for company benefits and would receive a W2 tax form at the end of the year.

More typically, the intern will be considered an independent contractor, ineligible for employee benefits, and will receive a 1099 tax form.

For the intern, it is usually beneficial to be considered a temporary employee, although this may be costlier for the host. The host may have head-count restrictions that prevent engagement of an intern as an employee.

Evidencing Professionalism

Irrespective of whether paid or not, the intern should commit sufficient time and determination to successfully complete the internship.

The host organization, likewise, should feel obligated to fulfil the training aspects of the position. This sense of obligation will be substantially greater when the intern is working on a volunteer basis.

Over-eagerness or fear of missing out may lead a student to take on too much. Having insufficient time, energy or creativity to apply to an internship will result in suboptimal performance. The intern will likely not create a good impression and fail to exercise their real skills and intellectual talents.

Whether paid or not, an internship is an opportunity to practice and to evidence professionalism.

Aspects to Consider

What considerations might I have before engaging an intern?

Prior to formally engaging an intern, it will be beneficial to consider a number of aspects.

Legal
The mechanics of engagement of an intern need to comply with the relevant labor laws.

Commitment
Intern, host and mentor are each making a significant commitment. At the outset, each party should be determined to make the project and the experience a success.

Safety
Any organization will take pride in its attention to safety and to staff wellbeing. It is expected that an intern will have limited or no exposure to industrial safety and security principles, measures and procedures. Particular attention then needs to be applied to initial safety training to minimize the risk of injury.

Confidentiality
Similarly, the intern will likely have limited knowledge of confidentiality requirements, of what types of information might be damaging to disclose, or of how an intellectual property position can be compromised by some form of public disclosure.

Liability and Insurance

Host liability for a paid intern is similar to that for any other staff member. A paid intern is generally covered for injury under the host's workers compensation insurance policy. Whether or not an unpaid intern is similarly covered does vary state to state although, typically, if the host controls the duties and scheduling of the unpaid intern the intern would generally be covered.[1]

Cost and Budgeting

The costs of a paid intern, whether on an employee or a contractor basis, need to be budgeted. Even though the amount may be relatively small, a budgeting requirement may necessitate significant advance planning.

Even for a volunteer intern, the host will incur outlays for use of a dedicated computer or other equipment, consumables and expenses, together with less obvious indirect costs such as of space. Significant time of the mentor and of peers and support functions will be applied.

Quality, Compliance, Procedures

The intern may require substantial formal or informal training to comply with the host's quality systems, safety and security requirements, and operational processes and procedures.

---

[1] For detailed advice for a particular state the reader is referred to the appropriate legal or insurance professional

Ongoing Obligation

The intern-host and, especially, the intern-mentor relationship rarely ends upon internship conclusion.

Intern's Subsequent Employer

Even when working at a junior level, an intern will be exposed to capabilities, information and work processes that the host will want to protect. An intern, by nature, is being primed for employment in the host's work sector, potentially even with a competitor. It is prudent to stress the criticality of non-disclosure, to underscore what types of information are considered proprietary, and even to plan the internship activities to avoid exposure to key trade secrets.

Finding an Internship Opportunity

How do I go about finding a suitable internship position?

There is no magic formula for securing an internship. It takes effort. It requires that different avenues are explored. It needs persistence, and it make take some luck.

Formal Academic Program

Several academic campuses offer an industrial business internship as a for-credit course. Usually, the campus has established relationships with local organizations which have agreed to host such internships. As the program is for academic credit, typically no compensation would be provided by the host organization. Although not formally on a 'volunteer' basis, similar expectations should apply as if it were.

Faculty Involved in Industry

Many campuses have teaching faculty who are associated in a part-time or advisory capacity with a company, or one or more lecturers or adjunct faculty who work in industry. Such faculty will typically be motivated to find opportunities for their students, either in their own company or in other companies with which they have connections.

Career Center

Academic career centers generally cultivate relationships with local companies. They might then provide a list of companies which have a history of intern engagements and be willing to make personal or networking introductions.

Position Postings

Especially for internship positions for which a specific project is identified, the company may advertise the availability of an internship on an academic career board. It is a 'may', though, as internship opportunities are often not advertised.

Web Search

Some companies will mention the possibility of an occasional internship on the careers or job posting section of their website. Even if a specific opportunity is not listed, mere mention of internships evidences the interest of the organization in considering such positions.

Advisory Board

Members of an academic advisory board to a given institution or department will likely respond to even a 'cold' contact (one that is unsolicited and from someone unknown or without introduction to the recipient) from a student in that department and facilitate an internship search.

Cold Contacts

The likelihood of success from a cold email may be low, but some professionals will take pains to read any such email. Several factors might elevate a cold email to the level of the recipient wanting to help or support the sender. High amongst them is an expression of keen interest in working in the recipient's company or, still more compelling, with the recipient specifically. A 'blanket' email (one that is broadcast to a lengthy recipient list without personalization) will rarely garner a reply.

Online Networks

Network connections, such as through LinkedIn, can be leveraged as a component of an internship search. LinkedIn can prove valuable both in seeking suitable hosts or mentors and as a means of learning about particular staff at a prospective host. The value in both regards increases with the number of established connections.

Industry Organizations

Companies in a given industry sector will likely belong to one or more local, state or national trade organizations. Part of the remit of such an industry organization is workforce development. The website, membership list or the staff at the organization may provide useful company leads and contacts.

Finding an Intern

How do I find suitable candidates for an internship position?

There is no single best source for identifying intern candidates, so that it is prudent to develop multiple channels.

Follow Up Discipline

Irrespective of the source of an internship application it is good practice to acknowledge receipt of each application and to keep each candidate loosely informed as to status. It is also beneficial to keep track of resumes and applications received for future reference. Applicants may augment the population of followers of the prospective host on social media.

Relatives of Team Members

High-performing employees will likely have high caliber daughters, sons and other relatives. Parents, especially, will be looking for ways for their offspring to gain work experience. When a parent and son or daughter work on the same site there are logistical benefits.

Community Connections

Networking connections into the communities populated by students who might be internship candidates and of people to whom such prospects will look for suggestions and recommendations will likely be fruitful.

Web Site Mention or Posting

An astute candidate will search the websites of a space of possible host organizations for occurrences of 'intern' or 'internship' and likely reach out to those making such mention, even if no specific opportunity is posted.

Word of Mouth

Demand for internships generally outstrips availability. Allowing word of willingness to serve as a host to percolate and encouraging alumni who have had positive experiences to pass on that message will progressively expand a host's catchment.

Presentation to Academic Audience

Most internship candidates will come from local campuses. For other than a large host organization with broad name recognition, there will be benefits to helping appropriate segments of the student body, as well as faculty and staff, become familiar with your organization. The campus career center will be keen to arrange a 'meet and greet' session with students. Student organizations might be interested to meet with an experienced industry figure. Contact information for such groups will be accessible through the campus website.

To serve as a host organization for an academic-credit internship will require being included in a list of suitable hosts provided to students. Such inclusion might follow contact with the program coordinators at each of the relevant departments on the campus.

Job Posting on Local Boards

Local colleges and universities provide job posting boards through the career services sections of their websites. These are viewed regularly by students so that an internship posting is expected to generate a robust response.

Many campuses also have less formal channels, such as Facebook groups organized by students, for sharing information about job and internship opportunities. An advantage of campus channels is that resulting applications will predominantly be from students or alumni from that selected campus.

Broader-catchment postings on sites that still cater to local audiences, such as Craigslist, may yield a substantial number of applications, although only a subset will likely be a match with the required profile. Responding diligently even to applicants that are not a suitable match can be a chore.

Postings Further Afield

Several sites have more of a national presence, even while supporting localized searching. Some of the better-known include internships.com, idealist.org, experience.com, mediabistro.com, hercampus.com, monster.com and indeed.com. Which online forums are most likely to be viewed by caliber candidates tends to evolve relatively quickly.

Even with local targeting, the broader the catchment of a site the broader the spectrum of applications is likely to be, necessitating an efficient screening process. Minimally, being very specific about requirements in the job description will discourage applications from those ill-fitting the required profile.

Network Leveraging

Soliciting intern applications or referrals through one's own professional network will help focus the space of applicants around a profile that is most suitable.

Past Intern Re-Engagement

A past intern might have evidenced a special aptitude. If a connection with the intern has been maintained, they may be available for a later engagement. In counterpoint, an intern might have found an internship so rewarding or enjoyable as to seek proactively a repeat.

Looking Ahead

A first internship hosting experience will likely sow the seeds for others. The more successful the experience and the more broadly such success is known the greater will be the reach for future candidates.

Interview

How should host and intern candidate approach an in-person interview and what should each aim to learn?

An in-person interview serves several purposes. It is a key step in the appraisal process by the mentor and by host staff. It will help establish what the intern hopes to achieve from the position. It will help the mentor devise or define details of the internship project. It will establish some measure of engagement of host staff additional to the mentor with the intern and with the project.

The candidate's focus will be on impressing each interviewer so as to be offered the position, but the interview is a two-way street. It allows a candidate to appraise the mentor and host staff, to gauge the company culture, and to set some measure of expectation for elements of the internship itself.

Host Side

People involved

Having a reasonable cross-section of peers and more senior staff participate in the interview process is beneficial to both host and intern. For each participant it will help build a sense of responsibility for the intern's success.

When several staff are involved in the interview process, it emphasizes the importance that the host ascribes to the internship program.

Guidance to each interviewer

Providing a simple feedback form to each interviewer can help structure each conversation. Such a structure encourages the interviewer to consider several aspects of the candidate's suitability. Without structure or guidance, an interview can end up being simply a chat, from which the outcome is solely an assessment of how well the interviewer either likes the candidate or considers the candidate will fit with the personalities of the other team members.

What to ask

When the intern candidate (or perhaps the interviewer) is not a native English speaker, a first order of business is to assess English language skills and the ability to communicate in spoken and written forms.

One way to approach an interview is to break it into sections, in each of which the emphasis will be on a different aspect (such sections being scripted by the feedback form).

First, the interviewer will develop a sense of the candidate's persona, the candidate's intelligence, personableness, dependability, responsibility, trustworthiness and professional maturity.

Second, the interviewer will probe the degree to which the candidate is coachable, how well they listen and absorb what they hear (or, instead, how eager they are to speak in a self-promotional way), how well they will respond to even subtle guidance.

Third will come an appraisal of the ability of the candidate to work independently, to assume responsibility for a project, to take ownership of issues and to be persistent in their resolve.

Fourth, the interviewer will want to assess the candidate's credentials, expertise and experience relative to the subject matter of the envisaged project. If the candidate's resume lists courses taken or specific skills the interviewer might ask detailed questions that test the veracity of the claimed competencies. If the project entails laboratory work, the level of proficiency with established experimentation techniques will be explored. If the project will entail working with a software package or writing macros or codes, the candidate may be put on the spot with a specific problem to solve using the package or coding.

Fifth, the mentor will want to know the details of the candidate's availability, over what period does it extend, for which days in each week, for which hours, and whether there are any scheduling constraints.

Finally, the level of the intern's interest in and enthusiasm for the host and for the internship is important. These may be gauged less by questions that the interviewer poses and more by the questions that are asked by the candidate.

Intern Candidate Side
Mentor and prospective colleagues
The level of enjoyment and fulfilment realized from a work experience depends to a large degree on people dynamics, on how well the individuals involved respect and trust each other, on how well each enjoys working with the others. The candidate will be assessing these aspects of the interviewing team, explicitly or implicitly.

Learning about the internship mentor and where they fit into the host organization is particularly important. Do they have mentoring experience? Do they have the time to commit on a regular basis? Will they be traveling frequently? How well regarded and how senior are they in the host organization?

References
Just as the host will likely check a candidate's references, the candidate can ask for contact information for one or more prior interns to ask about their experiences.

Constraints or particular wishes
At the interview, before a formal offer is made, it may be opportune to mention particular wishes or constraints. Perhaps the candidate has a two-week trip to Europe scheduled in the middle of the internship period for which time off would be needed, or the candidate may be particularly keen to gain experience with social media or some other aspect of the business.

Questions to pose

The candidate will want to express interest in and enthusiasm for the host and for the mentor, but only if genuine. This can be conveyed by asking pertinent questions, even if the candidate already knows the substance of many of the answers (based perhaps on having posed similar questions to interviewers earlier in the schedule).

Setting the stage

The interview is a first step in onboarding the successful candidate. Through the interview process the candidate begins to learn about the host's hierarchical structure (or lack of it), the work ethic and attention to detail of host staff, the extent of support and nurturing that the intern might expect, and the working arrangements with the mentor and with peers.

Securing the Position

How can I best position myself to be offered the internship I seek?

For an employee position, the appraisal concentrates on how well the candidate will be able to contribute. For an internship, of near-equal concern can be the degree to which the candidate will require hand-holding or might negatively impact other operations.

Connections

As with any staff position, a recommendation from someone known and respected by the host or by the mentor will carry a large weight. Mere mention of such a connection on a resume, provided it is genuine, will be an advantage.

Past Positions

Any job or internship experience will be viewed positively, as it implies professional responsibility, a work ethic, commitment and reliability. Prior jobs or internships evidencing that the candidate already has relevant skills or experience will substantially increase candidate's appeal.

Compliance and Fitting-in

There is a fine line between evidencing an ability to work independently and to assume responsibility for a project, and pursuing the program detailed by and under the guidance of the mentor. The project is a collaboration, that the mentor is also keen to progress. The candidate will benefit from evidencing an ability to dovetail into the management structure and to work well with colleagues.

Enthusiasm

All other things being equal, the intern candidate who is most enthusiastic about the opportunity in the host company will often be selected. It is persuasive to learn from a candidate that they are particularly eager to work for the host organization or, especially, with the mentor.

Logistical Items

How should I best go about onboarding an intern?

Follow up with References

An intern will be exposed to valuable company-confidential information and procedures. The intern may have access to information technology ("IT") systems. If the intern does not come from or through a respected contact, it is prudent to check one or two references.

Put a Formal Agreement in Place

It is important to substantiate provisions such as confidentiality, invention disclosure and assignment, and ownership of the outcomes of the intern's work (often termed 'work product') in a contract that will be executed by the intern and by the host.

The goals of the project for which the intern will be responsible, and any other expectations of the intern are beneficially also formally documented and agreed.

Assign and Set Expectations of the Mentor

The mentor should have a clear appreciation and acceptance of their role, responsibilities, and obligations. The value of an internship can be hugely enhanced by a mentor who proactively explores ways to enrich the intern's experience.

Protocols, Procedures and Modus Operandum

Company procedures are best discussed with the intern. The intern should be briefed on day-to-day working details, such as working hours, breaks, security, IT systems, work space and dress code. A tour of the facilities and introductions to other staff should be arranged.

Prioritize Formal Training

Safety training or briefing will be provided at the outset of the project. Company or research protocols to which the intern will be subject and training in standard operating procedures, laboratory notebook requirements and so on should be also be addressed early.

Structure Carefully the First Few Days

The first two or three weeks on the job are a critical period for any new team member. Within that initial period the company culture is imbibed, and an ongoing modus operandi is established.

A new intern addition will be enthusiastic to get established and to start contributing. That enthusiasm will diminish if there are bouts of inactivity. It is then recommended to plan a full first two weeks and to have frequent check-ins on acclimatization and progress.

A new intern will interact with several colleagues, the closest of will beneficially be involved in the initial orientation process.

Legal Mechanics[2]

What legal issues should I be aware of?

Federal and state employment laws provide a slate of protections for employees (there are number of online sources; see, for example, https://www.dol.gov/general/aboutdol/majorlaws). The Fair Labor Standards Act ("FLSA") provides that individuals who are considered 'employed' must be paid minimum wage and overtime compensation.

An intern in the 'for-profit' sector is considered employed unless six conditions provided by the U.S. Department of Labor, for which details and comments are provided following, are all satisfied (https://www.dol.gov/whd/regs/compliance/whdfs71.htm). Many states, including California, follow these federal labor laws.

1. The Internship Position is Educational in Nature

The position will provide practical training. The intern should gain hands-on experience with activities of the host organization, such as use of equipment, experimentation, business processes or procedures. This training and experience will then position the intern for subsequent employment in the host's industry sector, potentially even with the host.

---

[2] The reader should refer directly to the relevant labor laws or to an employment attorney for definitive advice for a specific case.

2. The Internship is for the Benefit the Intern

It should be clear that the internship is designed for the benefit of the intern. Developing an internship program specifically around the interests and skills of the intern, or around skills that the intern most hopes to acquire, can satisfy this requirement. The host will incur costs in onboarding, supervising and training the intern. The host should reasonably expect some benefit or some prospect of future benefit.

3. The Intern does not Displace a Regular Employee

The work of the intern would not otherwise be undertaken by another employee, or at least by another employee over a similar period.

This requires planning. For the internship to be most useful from a training perspective and to ensure that the intern's work is of interest to the mentor and to work colleagues, the intern project should be in an area central to the operations or interests of the host.

4. The Internship Provides no Immediate Advantage for the Host

It would make no business sense for a host to engage an intern were there zero prospect of any value to the host. Such value, though, is anticipated as a future benefit. The intern is not being engaged to serve an immediate need or business opportunity.

5. There is no Promise of Future Employment

The intern will neither expect nor be entitled to any form of employment following completion of the internship. However, should the intern perform well, and should a suitable position become available following completion of the internship, the intern will inevitably be well-positioned as a candidate.

6. It is Clearly Understood that the Position is Unpaid

The intern will not receive any payment for the internship activities or for time spent on such activities. If the intern incurs pre-approved expenses (such as materials, travel or local expenses, external class attendance), though, provision for reimbursement should be made.

The agreement for both host and intern to adhere to these six provisions is conveniently incorporated into the internship agreement that both will sign. One of the host's obligations is to ensure that the mentor, or indeed any other employee who might direct the work of the intern, is aware of these conditions.

Because of these requirements, the type of project that is assigned to a volunteer intern will often be different from that which would be assigned on a paid basis. In this regard, an internship undertaken for academic credit will likely fall, guideline-wise, into the unpaid category.

Independent Contractor versus Employee

An employee enjoys a range of benefits and protections under the applicable labor laws, including provision of workers' compensation insurance, eligibility for state unemployment insurance benefits, minimum wage and overtime provisions, and antidiscrimination protections. An employee is also subject to withholding of state and federal payroll taxes.

As of quite recently in California, a simple three-part test is applied to determine whether an individual engaged by a company is an independent contractor or an employee. An independent contractor (a) is free from the control and direction of the company in connection with performing the work, (b) performs work that is outside the usual course of the company's business, and (c) is customarily engaged in an independently established occupation of the same nature as the work being performed for the company.

Documentation

What sort of agreement should be implemented between a host and an intern?

As with any formal agreement between parties, there is little excuse for not properly documenting the structure and expectations for the internship.

Confidentiality, Intellectual Property and Ownership

The internship agreement to be executed by the intern and by the host representative should, as with any employee agreement, include provisions for confidentiality, invention ownership, and intellectual property assignment. It would be unusual for the intern to retain any rights to inventions or other intellectual property generated during their internship tenure.

Termination

The host will want to retain the option to terminate the internship at any time, generally without notice, or, minimally, to terminate upon breach of the internship agreement. The host will also ask the intern for a period of notice prior to termination by the intern, especially if the intern is on a paid basis and supporting a key host program.

No Conflict or Competition

It is reasonable to require an intern to inform the host should the intern intend to work with another company operating in the same business space as the host company. The host will have the option then to restructure or to terminate the internship. It is challenging to enforce any form of non-compete provision with a duration that extends beyond the internship period itself. In contrast, non-disclosure and non-use provisions will have longer-term

ooo

enforceability. Likewise, a non-solicitation clause would typically extend to one or two years beyond the internship period to prevent an intern from poaching host employees.

Compensation and Expense Reimbursement

The details of any compensation to be paid, or not, should be detailed, together with the responsibilities for withholding or payment of taxes. How any compensation will be reported to the tax authorities, whether under a W2 or a 1099, is usefully provided.

Whether expenses incurred will be reimbursed and the mechanics of arranging for same can be listed.

Insurance

The intern should acknowledge eligibility, or not as the case may be, for coverage under host's workers compensation insurance policy.

Project Details

Particularly for a volunteer internship, it is beneficial to document the duration planned for the internship, the goal and the sub-objectives of the internship project, and the expectations on both the intern and the mentor.

Value in Review

Even though an internship agreement might be crafted in formal legal terminology, it is valuable for the intern to review and understand the agreement, and to have the opportunity, as a learning exercise, to ask questions about its structure, provisions and language. It will likely not be the last contract of this type that the intern will be asked to execute.

Recipe for Success

What components are key to maximizing the likelihood of success in an internship?

Internships and internship experiences are diverse. There is no universal formula for success that addresses the full spectrum of potential hosts and possible projects. The following guidelines were developed to structure an internship which is (i) project based, (ii) pursued largely independently by the intern, and (iii) not subject to specially-constraining requirements (such as shadowing or the need to work closely with the mentor or with another host employee, a need for training with special equipment or instrumentation, familiarity with complex techniques or quality-controlled procedures, or working with multiple team members on a project that is fluidly distributed).

1. Two is an Ideal Number

Without active supervision, it can be hard for an intern to sustain momentum. If the regular discussion sessions with the mentor are infrequent, such as weekly, momentum is more likely to be maintained if the 'intern' is a team of two. Rather than being an impediment, there can be advantages should the internship partners not know each other prior to working together on the project.

In a team of three, responsibility for progress or task completion can become ambiguous. A team of four or more is still more unwieldy. Unless all are engaged full-time, coordinating meetings and activities is a challenge.

2. The Project Theme Resonates with Interests

The enthusiasm and motivation will be greater when the intern has a pre-established interest in the general area of the project. If the mentor is working to articulate a suitable project, such an interest might be gleaned from the intern's resume or during the interview.

3. The Goal is Clearly Articulated and Measurable

Having a clear goal that the intern is responsible for achieving ensures focus. It prevents drift, a state in which the intern is committing time but is not motivatingly engaged. The goal should be challenging, but tractable. As a suggested guide, averaged over ten different internships, the full goal should be realized in perhaps 30-40% of the cases.

4. Steps to Achieve the Goal are Detailed

Mapping intermediate steps towards achieving the project goal as measurable sub-objectives provides structure and shorter-term goals. Even should the overall project goal not be attained, realization of certain of the sub-objectives will provide a measure of satisfaction to the intern and of benefit to the host.

5. A Set Duration is Defined

A timeline and an end date are agreed. A duration of around three months can be optimal. The intern and the mentor may seek to continue work on the project after the agreed end date, but it is preferable to complete a first project close-out and then to establish a new project with a fresh three-month goal and appropriate sub-objectives.

6. There is a Formal Project Agreement

A mutual understanding is rarely understood mutually unless it is agreed in writing. The project goal and sub-objectives should be documented. The project agreement will also memorialize ownership of project data and results (and any associated intellectual property), confidentiality, adherence to host procedures and so on.

7. Supervision is Sufficient but not Excessive

A key determinant of job satisfaction is empowerment, the recognition by the employee that they are in charge of their schedule, that they are responsible for their progress and for their mistakes. This empowerment is, of course, subject to adherence to necessary host procedures and practices. If a mentor is overly involved, such micromanagement will diminish both the enthusiasm of the intern and the benefits of the project to both intern and to host.

8. Intern and Mentor Discuss on a Regular Schedule

Without regular meetings between the intern and the host, momentum is lost and, once lost, is rarely regained. Such meetings allow progress to be reviewed, issues to be considered, and priorities for the next period to be agreed. The intern will be motivated to make substantive progress in time for the next scheduled meeting.

9. The Intern Maintains Detailed Notes

Keeping detailed and well-organized notes will enable a subsequent intern or other host staff member to build further on the intern's progress and results. It is in the interest of each of the intern, the host and the mentor that the intern's efforts have the possibility of durable impact. The discipline of efficient note-keeping may prove to be a lasting professional skill.

10. The Project Ends with a Closeout Session

A closeout session, such as where the intern presents their project to a host or external audience, provides a satisfying conclusion. It enables an assessment of the level of goal achievement. It helps to disseminate information on the intern's contributions. It provides a polarizing objective on which the intern can focus.

Continuing Connection

Why should the connection of the intern with the mentor and the host be maintained even after an internship is concluded?

In addition to professional friendships that are established between work colleagues, a familial sense of responsibility for the intern may well develop, especially for the mentor.

Interest in Progress

A mentor who has worked to help an intern realize best benefits will be at least curious and, very likely, interested to hear how the intern develops professionally. Learning which aspects of an internship contribute in a lasting way to such development will enable the mentor to be still more effective in approaching future mentorships.

Networking

Our network tends to be strongest with our peers, or with those of similar age, responsibility level and career progression. The professional networks of the mentor and that of the intern will likely have little overlap. The intersection of the two may lead to interesting new connection opportunities.

Future Opportunities

An intern who has excelled in a project will be a preferred candidate for a future position with the host. An intern may also be interested to pursue a subsequent internship with the same host or mentor.

References and Recommendations

An implicit responsibility of the mentor or the host is to provide references or recommendations for the intern upon request. An exceptional mentor will go further and work proactively to identify opportunities and to make introductions or referrals.

Referrals

An intern who has had a positive experience with a host will recommend the host to future internship prospects.

Ongoing Engagement

The host may invite an alumnus intern, being part of the larger 'company family', to future events, such as company socials. The alumnus may also be interested to participate as part of a host organization presence at outreach activities, such as science or business fairs, or visits to local middle and high schools.

Example Projects

What are some exemplary internship project goals?

The following are the documented goals for a number of recent internships. All were concluded, with varying levels of success, within the agreement timeline of, typically, 2-4 months. Each project was undertaken by a team of two or, less frequently, one or three, and in one case four.

General

Shepherd the draft manuscript of 'Making Your Mark with a Scientific Presentation' through to first phase completion and review by five individuals.

Promote the invited symposium 'Entrepreneurship - the quest for start-up success based on research advances' at the March Meeting of the American Physical Society to maximize attendance and impact.

Develop a strategic plan in the format of a PowerPoint presentation for establishing the greater San Diego region as a recognized skin hub within five years.

Big Data

Implement a capability for searching across the majority of academic technology transfer offices for availability of intellectual property relating to given search terms.

Design, implement & validate a maintainable in-house software system for finding and weighting occurrences of compounds and compound combinations in large text datasets, especially of patents

Microbiome

Recommend the ten most interesting investment prospects amongst early phase companies pursuing products or services in the microbiome space.

Complete a compelling and actionable plan for a new endeavor directed to making early-stage investments in and facilitating the progress of microbiome companies.

Contract Manufacturing

Build a compelling business plan as a PowerPoint slide deck for a new contract development and manufacturing organization dedicated to topical pharmaceutical products.

Elder Care

Develop a compelling business brief for a year 2020 elder care facility.

Topical Pharmaceutical Products

Present ten unmet medical needs addressable by topical or transdermal administration of a small molecule drug that are commercially-appealing targets.

Present compelling business and technical cases for development of three new oral thin film products, including a summary of capabilities needed to complete innovation of such formulation products.

Implement a verified capability for measuring delivery of an active into the eye from a topically-applied formulation.

Develop compelling scientific and business cases for two new topically-applied cannabinoid products, together with, for a regulated drug product, the medical rationale.

Establish a broadly useful protocol for ranking the esthetics of topically applied formulations.

Identify and detail convincingly how a contract research organization might take best business advantage of the latest developments in skin tissue culturing and printing.

Identify the top thirty skin-applied product innovations that are in development and devise three prospective new products with commercial appeal.

Assemble a database of the key molecular characteristics of drug products approved by the US Food and Drug Administration for transdermal or topical administration and propose two prospective new transdermal drug products.

Crowdsourced Predictions in the Energy Sector

Develop a pitch for each of two opportunities in the energy market sector that will be compelling as an application of a crowdsourcing prediction technology.

Technology-based Business Opportunities

Develop a business plan as a slide deck for a new company in the general microfluidics space that is sufficiently compelling that the intern will want to commit to founding the company.

Elaborate one or more viable technical approaches to a commercial product that would indicate when a drink is spiked with a date-rape drug.

Identify new technologies to improve the efficiency of the rum production process and make the business case for a new endeavor that could achieve commercial success through leveraging one or more of such technologies.

Technology Transfer Offices
Assemble a database of all technology transfer offices in the US, Australia, UK, Germany, France and Spain and complete searches across all such offices for three stipulated technologies.

Wastewater Treatment
Develop a high-level summary of principal wastewater streams and of treatment methods and identify the most appealing commercial applications of a specific new water treatment technology.

Technology for Underdeveloped Nations
Accumulate a list of ten widely-differing needs in a pre-selected underdeveloped region or country with, for each, a concept that might enable the need to be addressed in the short term and develop a compelling game plan for pursuit of the lead concept.

Stem Cell Technology
Collate information on companies in the stem cell field, scout ten recent scientific and technological developments which represent new business opportunities and develop a compelling five-slide pitch for the three opportunities of greatest appeal.

Funding for Non-profits
Research internet and social networking technologies that local non-profit organizations use to solicit and attract funding and propose three innovative business models by which funding for a local non-profit life sciences organization might be realized.

Music Composition

Assemble information on organizations, technologies and software to facilitate music composition and sound generation and develop the concept for a new company to pursue such capabilities.

Software for Molecular Simulation and Sales Support

Summarize the strengths, weaknesses, opportunities, and threats of companies offering molecular simulation software or contract services and propose a preferred business model for a new company to be created in this business space.

Develop the bases for estimating the market potential and initial sales prospecting for a smartphone app deployed as a life sciences sales support tool.

Career Development Support

Establish an efficient and extensible MySQL implementation of a career trajectory database system, with user-friendly population and query tools, suitable for projected use over a two-year period.

Develop a compelling pitch for a professional life scientist organization to place and develop staff and facilitate individual career progressions.

Educational and Training Programs
Appraise key topics in molecular diagnostics and personalized medicine and develop the curriculum, with draft course materials, for a one-day corporate program to brief non-scientist professionals in these topics.

Assess current biotechnology informational programs offered online, identify gaps, and assemble a database of prospective clients for educational programs addressing such gaps.

Business and Corporate Development
Assemble an actionable and prioritized list of merger targets or potential acquirers of a stipulated early-phase company.

Develop a comprehensive summary of life sciences innovations and technologies from Cuba relating to skin applied products and propose one such innovation suitable for commercialization in the US.

Identify and assess all significant competitors to the services business of a stipulated company.

Develop a database of all companies in India that might be a prospective client or partner of a stipulated service provider, develop a scoring system to rank such prospects, and devise an initial contacting and follow-up strategy for the top ten such prospects.

Devise a strategy and tactics suitable for ensuring that any prospective client of a stipulated company is both aware of such company's offerings and thinks first of engaging such company whenever a relevant need arises.

Product Planning

Develop the basis to support decisions relative to pursuit of three stipulated product opportunities.

Biological Tissue Sourcing

Research the safety and quality requirements for handling fresh human skin samples and appraise prospective regional suppliers of such tissues.

Upon Completion

How should an internship end?

An internship had a distinct beginning, and a middle. It should also have an orderly and satisfying end.

Summary Session with Feedback

A summary presentation by the intern is a tidy way to wrap-up the project. It provides the intern with the opportunity to present to a small host audience, summarizing what and how they have done. It provides the host audience with the chance to recognize the extent of the intern's progress and contributions. Knowing that such a presentation is scheduled helps to focus the intern's thinking and efforts. A summary presentation may also be a prelude to a farewell social event, such as a lunch.

Exit Interview

A formal exit interview, supported by an exit form, provides the opportunity to remind the intern about ongoing provisions relating to confidentiality and intellectual property, to ensure return of tangible host items, such as laboratory notebooks and keys, and to trigger other actions, such as cancelling of computer access or closing of an email account.

Staying in Touch

Both mentor and host will want to maintain current contact information for the graduating intern.

Acknowledgements

Who should be recognized and thanked for their contributions to this work?

Brief though it may be, this book would not have developed to the point of publication without substantial help from several colleagues and friends.

Still more importantly, I am grateful to the many individuals who have shared internship experiences and insights with me. Only a small portion of what I have learned from each of you is included here.

About the Author

 In addition to facilitating placement of interns with other supervisors, groups and companies, John M Newsam has personally supervised more than seventy interns over the past few years, predominantly undergraduates, recent graduates or postgraduates and, occasionally, high school students. The majority of these internship projects have been based in the Southern California region but, under special and infrequent circumstances, also elsewhere.

Alumni from these internships have gone on to take up professorships and other faculty appointments, medical, pharmacy and dental professional positions, or various roles in industry and business. A LinkedIn group, 'The Minnow Tank', was established by one alumnus to encourage networking amongst this group of alumni.

Made in the USA
San Bernardino, CA
31 January 2019